Animal Predators

J O S H   G R E G O R Y

Children's Press®
An Imprint of Scholastic Inc.

Content Consultant
Dr. Stephen S. Ditchkoff
Professor of Wildlife Sciences
Auburn University
Auburn, Alabama

Library of Congress Cataloging-in-Publication Data
Gregory, Josh, author.
 Animal predators / Josh Gregory.
    pages cm. — (A true book)
 Summary: "Learn all about nature's most incredible predators, from how different species hunt
to what animals they prey upon"— Provided by publisher.
 Audience: Ages 9–12.
 Audience: Grades 4–6.
 Includes bibliographical references and index.
 ISBN 978-0-531-21546-3 (library binding : alk. paper) — ISBN 978-0-531-21583-8 (pbk. : alk.
paper)
1. Predatory animals—Juvenile literature. 2. Predation (Biology)—Juvenile literature. I. Title. II.
Series: True book.
 QL758.G74 2016
 591.5'3—dc23   2014049199

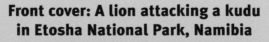

**Front cover: A lion attacking a kudu
in Etosha National Park, Namibia**

**Back cover: An osprey snatching
a trout in Finland**

Find the Truth!

Everything you are about to read is true *except* for one of the sentences on this page.

Which one is **TRUE**?

T or F   Predators are usually very large animals.

T or F   Some shrew species use venom when attacking their prey.

Find the answers in this book.

Contents

1 On the Hunt

Why do animals kill and eat each other? 7

2 Forests and Fields

What animals use their tongues to snatch prey? . . 13

THE BIG TRUTH!

Predator Invasion

How can predators cause problems when they
are introduced to new places? 24

3 Death From Above

What makes birds such effective
hunters? 27

A pack of wolves attacks its prey.

4 Under the Sea

How do deep-sea predators lure in unsuspecting prey? **35**

True Statistics **44**

Resources **45**

Important Words **46**

Index **47**

About the Author **48**

There are more than 600 venomous snake species on Earth.

CHAPTER 1

On the Hunt

A shrew catches and eats a worm, then scampers across the forest floor in search of more food. Soon, the unsuspecting shrew is bitten and swallowed whole by a well-hidden snake. Hours later, a hawk swoops down from the sky and snatches the snake in its sharp **talons**. Though these animals have very different lifestyles, they all have one thing in common. They are **predators**.

Red-shouldered hawks wait on a perch until they spot their next meal.

Munching on Meat

Predators are animals that hunt and kill other animals as a source of food. Some dine on insects and spiders. Others make a meal of a large, powerful mammal. Some predators are carnivores. This means their diet consists almost entirely of other animals. Predators can also be omnivores. This means they eat both plants and animals.

Grizzly bears are omnivores. They eat roots, berries, and seeds in addition to fish and other animals.

All predators have a place in their ecosystems. An ecosystem is a complex web of relationships between all the plants and animals in a place. A tree uses water, sunlight, and nutrients from soil to grow. A number of

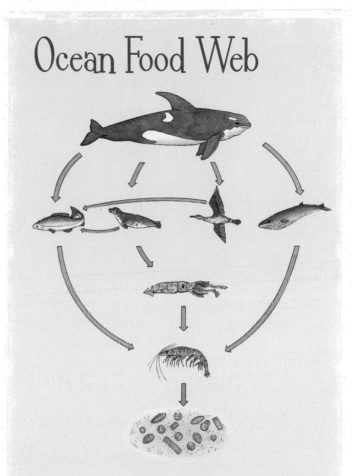

Ocean Food Web

In this chart, arrows point from each ocean predator to the animal or animals it eats.

animals might rely on that tree's leaves, fruit, and other parts for food. Those animals become **prey** for local predators. Some predators are also prey for even stronger predators.

Every species has an important role in its ecosystem, from plants and prey animals to predators.

Keeping a Balance

This web of predators and prey is a necessary part of a healthy environment. Without predators, prey animals would grow too numerous. They would need more food of their own than was available. There would not be enough space for them. This would in turn affect the populations of other local plant and animal **species**. The balance of the entire ecosystem would be thrown off.

Unique Challenges

Predators occupy a diverse range of habitats. They live in the dense jungles of South America and the sprawling grasslands of Africa. They hunt across the icy expanses of the Arctic and in the world's hottest, driest deserts. Some of them probably even live in your own backyard. Because they live in such different places and have different diets, each animal has its own way of hunting prey.

Predators face a variety of challenges—such as this hedgehog's pointy spines—when trying to catch prey.

An arctic fox leaps headfirst into
the snow to catch prey.

CHAPTER 2

Forests and Fields

Prey animals can have a wide range of defenses to protect against attacks. Even small, seemingly harmless creatures can be dangerous or difficult to hunt. As a result, many predators have developed specialized methods of capturing their meals. Some are strong and fast, while others are quick thinkers. Some even have special body parts or natural abilities that make them effective hunters.

Arctic foxes can pinpoint where a mouse is hiding under the snow by listening.

Pack Predators

Teamwork is important to some predators. Perhaps the best example of this is the gray wolf. Wolves travel in close-knit groups called packs. When a wolf sees or smells possible prey, it howls to call other pack members to help it. Working together, a small group of wolves can chase down and kill huge animals such as moose and bison.

Average wolf packs have 6 to 8 members. Some packs include more than 20 wolves.

14

It takes more than one lion to take down a buffalo.

Lions often work together, too. These powerful hunters can attack and kill any type of animal they meet in their African home. They prey on everything from apes and zebras to hippopotamuses and even elephants. Lions hunt by sneaking up as close as possible to prey. Then they chase the animal down, lunging at its neck and biting with powerful jaws. For very large or fast prey, multiple lions surround the animal to overpower it.

Polar bears can smell prey from more than 0.6 miles (1 kilometer) away.

Lying in Wait

Patience is an important skill for many predators. A polar bear's diet consists almost entirely of seals. When seals dive into the icy Arctic water, they must eventually come up for air. One way a polar bear hunts is by sniffing out gaps in the ice where seals surface. Then the bear waits, motionless. When a seal's head pokes up, the bear grabs it and pulls it out of the water.

Built-In Tools

Certain predators rely on special physical features to catch prey. Anteaters have long, narrow faces and sticky tongues. These animals poke their faces like straws into anthills and termite burrows. Then they use their tongues to scoop up mouthfuls of insects.

Frogs also have long, sticky tongues. They shoot these powerful tools out to snatch unsuspecting prey. Large frogs can use their tongues to grab anything from insects to **rodents** to birds—and even other frogs!

A frog leaps at a fly, trying to catch the prey with its sticky tongue.

17

Small and Speedy

The tiger beetle is a fast-moving insect found in many parts of the world. It can run at speeds of up to 5 miles (8 km) per hour. This might not seem very fast, but the tiger beetle is very small. Its top speed allows it to travel 120 times the length of its body per second! This means the tiger beetle is actually one of the fastest animals on Earth. It uses this incredible speed to chase down its fellow insects and grab them in its jaws.

Tiger beetles move so fast that everything turns into a blur for them. They often have to pause to look where they are going!

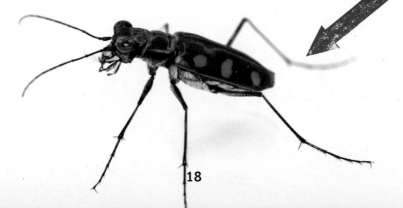

Trapped in a Web

Spiders use intricate webs to capture prey. A spider builds its trap using silk. Silk is produced in **glands** in the spider's body. It is very strong and sticky. Different spider species build their webs in different shapes, but most webs work in a similar way. An unsuspecting insect runs into the web and becomes stuck. It also vibrates the web. This informs the spider that prey has been caught. The predator can then rush over and eat.

Chimps make "sponges" by chewing up leaves, dipping them into puddles, and drinking the water the leaves soak up.

A chimpanzee picks termites off a twig.

Sticks and Stones

Scientists once believed that humans were the only animals that knew how to make and use tools. However, some clever predators can use simple objects such as rocks or twigs to capture prey. For example, chimpanzees sometimes poke sticks into insect nests and eat the insects that climb onto the sticks. Some researchers have even seen chimps sharpen sticks. They use these sticks to spear small animals living inside hollow trees!

Get a Grip

Though many predators rely on teeth or claws to kill prey, snakes called constrictors are strong enough to simply squeeze prey to death. A constrictor hides and waits for prey to come close. Then the snake strikes out and grips the prey in its mouth. The snake wraps its body around the prey and squeezes. The prey dies because it can't breathe. Then the snake opens its mouth wide and swallows its meal whole.

This boa constrictor has captured three opossums.

Vicious and Venomous

Poison is an important part of hunting for many predators. The poison, or venom, either **paralyzes** or kills prey. Venom is produced in special glands. These glands are often located near a predator's teeth. For many of these animals, the venom drips along the teeth. In some snakes, venom flows through a pair of hollow fangs. Either way, the venom enters an animal's body when the predator bites. Other predators, such as scorpions, deliver poison through stingers.

Rattlesnakes can control how much venom they use on a victim.

An animal usually dies within 24 hours of being bitten by a komodo dragon.

You probably know that many types of snakes, insects, and spiders are famous for their venomous bites. But did you know that certain mammals, including some species of shrews and moles, also have poisonous bites? The reptile known as the komodo dragon has **bacteria** in its mouth. When it bites, the bacteria cause a deadly infection in prey. The komodo dragon then follows the dying prey and waits for the infection to finish its job.

THE **BIG** TRUTH!

Predator Invasion

Ecosystems are finely balanced. When humans introduce a new predator into an area, this balance is upset. Invasive predators can cause big problems for native species.

Cane Toads

In the 19th century, humans began bringing these large toads from the Americas to other parts of the world. They hoped the toads would control local pest populations. Cane toads have poisonous skin, which keeps many predators from eating them. Without predators to keep them in check, toad populations have grown out of control. In places such as Australia, native species now compete with the deadly toads for food.

American Mink

Humans brought minks from North America to other parts of the world in the 20th century. They wanted to use mink fur to make clothing. However, some of these minks got loose and thrived in the wild. Today, certain types of rodents, birds, and other animals that the minks eat are disappearing in some places.

Pythons

Burmese pythons were brought as pets to the United States from Asia. U.S. python owners sometimes became unable or unwilling to care for the snakes

and set them free in the wild. The snakes thrived in some places, particularly in Florida. There are now thousands of these deadly snakes roaming wild there. They prey on Florida's wildlife and compete for food with alligators and other native predators.

CHAPTER 3

Death From Above

Not all predators are limited to moving along the ground in search of prey. Birds and other flying animals can take to the skies and look down on the creatures below. This allows them to survey a much wider area than predators on the ground can. It also lets them launch surprise attacks from above, where prey might not spot them until it's too late.

Sea eagles sometimes dive underwater to catch fish.

A bald eagle snatches a fish from the water.

In rare cases, bald eagles have attacked prey as large as deer!

The Raptor Strikes

Predatory birds called raptors are some of the most dangerous hunters in the sky. Eagles, falcons, and hawks are raptors. They have excellent vision. They can spot even small animals moving around below. They catch prey by diving and using their sharp talons to grab the prey from the ground or water.

Most of the time, raptors carry their prey to a nearby perch. Then they use their sharp, strong beaks to tear off pieces to eat. Sometimes, though, these birds attack prey that is too big to carry. The golden eagle is known for attacking mountain goats. It grabs the goat in its talons and drags it off the edge of a cliff. The goat dies when it hits the ground, and then the eagle can eat.

A martial eagle fights with a warthog in Africa.

Night Flight

Owls are great hunters at night. Their large eyes are perfect for seeing well in the dark. Owls also have very sensitive hearing. An owl can hear a mouse's footsteps dozens of feet away. Some owls fly around looking for prey. Others simply perch in trees and wait for prey to pass beneath them. Like other raptors, they dive and snatch prey in their talons. Then they carry it back to a perch before eating.

A saw-whet owl extends its claws to catch a mouse.

Brown pelicans are the only pelicans that dive at prey from the air.

Scooping Up a Snack

Pelicans have stretchy pouches in their throats, just under their beaks. These pouches work like a net. A pelican opens its beak and scoops fish out of the water. The fish are trapped in the pouch and swallowed whole. Most pelicans work together. They swim in groups and drive fish into areas where they can be caught easily. However, one species hunts by making steep dives from the sky to scoop up its prey from the water.

A robin pulls a worm from the ground.

A Beakful of Bugs

Many smaller bird species are also predators. Woodpeckers use their strong, pointy beaks to drill holes in trees and reach the bugs inside. Small, quick fliers such as swifts and swallows use their speed to snatch insects out of the air. Robins look and listen for worms moving around near the surface of the soil. They then reach down and snatch their meals out of the ground.

Mammals on the Wing

Bats are the only kind of mammal that can fly. While some bat species eat fruit, most prey on flying insects. These insect eaters usually hunt at night. A bat locates prey by sending out sound waves. The sounds bounce off prey and other objects and return to the bat. This tells the bat about its prey's location, direction of movement, and speed. With this information, a bat can snatch insects mid-flight!

There are more than 1,200 different bat species.

CHAPTER 4

Under the Sea

Beneath the surface of the world's waters lives a diverse range of animals unlike anything on land. These animals range from **microscopic** creatures to the largest species living today. Some are common sights along coastal areas. Others dwell far below the surface in places humans have never even seen. Just like on land, many of these animals are deadly predators.

Sharks have been around for about 400 million years.

Shark Attack

One of the ocean's deadliest and most well-known hunters is the great white shark. These huge sharks have several rows of sharp, jagged teeth in their mighty jaws. They use their speed and strength to launch surprise attacks on prey. As it speeds toward a target, a great white shark opens its mouth wide and bites down. Most prey die almost immediately after this first bite.

A great white shark breaks the water's surface as it catches its prey.

Like bats, dolphins send out sound waves to help them locate prey and avoid obstacles.

Deadly Dolphins

Dolphins are known for their intelligence and playfulness. However, they are also skilled hunters. Like wolves, dolphins often hunt in groups. These groups are called pods. Pod members often hunt by swimming in a circle around a large group of fish. They take turns eating the fish and circling in order to keep the prey from escaping.

Water filters from a humpback whale's mouth after the whale has gathered a mouthful of krill.

Filter Feeding

The ocean's biggest whales are larger than any animals on land. In fact, the blue whale is possibly the largest animal to ever live. Though enormous, these whales mostly eat tiny shrimp-like animals called krill. A blue whale eats by opening its mouth and sucking in water. When it closes its mouth, the water is squeezed out. Any krill or other small animals that were in the water become stuck in special bristles in the whale's mouth.

Glowing in the Dark

Parts of the ocean are so far beneath the surface that there is no sunlight. In this darkness, some deep-sea creatures make their own light. Many of them are predators that use their light to lure in prey. The deep-sea anglerfish (below) has a glowing lure on top of its head. Other animals see the light and think it is easy prey. When they come close enough, the anglerfish opens its wide mouth and captures its meal.

Tangled in Tentacles

Have you ever seen a jellyfish? These sea creatures are often beautiful. They can also be deadly. A jellyfish's mouth is located on the bottom of its body. Tentacles hang down all around the mouth. These tentacles hold venom.

As the jellyfish moves through the water, prey bump into the tentacles and are stung. The stings stop the prey from moving. The jellyfish uses body parts called oral arms to carry the prey to its mouth.

A box jellyfish slowly eats a fish.

A crocodile attacks a herd of wildebeest trying to cross the Mara River in Kenya.

Mighty Mouths

Some predators hunt both in the water and on land. Crocodiles live around lakes, rivers, swamps, and other water habitats. Much of their diet is fish. However, larger species also attack land animals such as zebras and antelope. To do this, a crocodile hides submerged near the water's edge. When an animal bends down for a drink, the crocodile bursts forward. It bites the animal's head or neck and drags it underwater to drown it.

Leopard seals often hunt penguins and smaller seals.

Diving Deep

Seals are mammals that split their time between land and water. They prey on fish, squid, and a variety of other water animals. They do this by diving deep underwater. One species, the Weddell seal, has been known to reach depths of up to 1,969 feet (600 meters). Because they spend so much time underwater, seals are good at holding their breath. A deep dive might take anywhere from 20 minutes to more than an hour!

A Small Sample

These predators are but a few of the countless species living today. In almost every environment imaginable, there are animals using a range of methods to catch their dinner. There is still plenty to learn about these animals and their hunting techniques. In mysterious places like the ocean depths, there might even be whole new predator species to discover. Will you be the one to uncover this new knowledge? ★

Submersibles like this one allow researchers to observe animals far below the ocean's surface.

True Statistics

Average weight of a blue whale: 150 tons

Number of bat species: More than 1,200

Number of wolves in an average pack: 6 to 8

Distance a polar bear can smell prey from: 0.6 mi. (1 km)

Length of an adult lion's canine teeth: 3.9 in. (10 cm)

Wingspan of a bald eagle: 8 ft. (2.4 m)

Depth a Weddell seal can reach while diving: 1,969 ft. (600 m)

Did you find the truth?

F Predators are usually very large animals.

T Some shrew species use venom when attacking their prey.

Resources

Books

Gregory, Josh. *Owls*. New York: Children's Press, 2013.

Marsico, Katie. *Sharks*. New York: Children's Press, 2012.

Raatma, Lucia. *Pythons*. New York: Children's Press, 2013.

Zeiger, Jennifer. *Lions*. New York: Children's Press, 2012.

Visit this Scholastic Web site for more information on animal predators:
★ www.factsfornow.scholastic.com
Enter the keywords **Animal Predators**

Important Words

bacteria (bak-TEER-ee-uh) — microscopic, single-celled living things that exist everywhere and that can either be useful or harmful

glands (GLANDZ) — organs in the body that produce or release natural chemicals

invasive (in-VAY-siv) — describing a plant or animal that is introduced to a new habitat and may cause that habitat harm

microscopic (mye-kruh-SKAH-pik) — extremely small

paralyzes (PAR-uh-lize-iz) — makes (an animal) unable to move or feel a part of the body

predators (PREH-duh-turz) — animals that live by hunting other animals for food

prey (PRAY) — an animal that's hunted by another animal for food

rodents (ROH-duhnts) — mammals with large, sharp front teeth that are constantly growing and are used for gnawing things

species (SPEE-sheez) — one of the groups into which animals and plants of the same genus are divided

talons (TAL-uhnz) —claws of a bird such as an eagle, hawk, or falcon

Index

Page numbers in **bold** indicate illustrations.

anglerfish, **39**
anteaters, 17
arctic foxes, **12**, 13

balance, 10, 24
bats, **33**
bears, **8**, **16**
buffalo, **15**

cane toads, **24**
carnivores, 8
chimpanzees, **20**
crocodiles, **41**

dolphins, **37**

eagles, **26**, 27, **28**, **29**
ecosystems, **9**, **10**, 24

fish, **8**, **28**, 31, **37**, **39**, **40**, 41, 42
food webs, **9**, 10
frogs, **17**

habitats, 11, 41
hawks, **6**, 7, 28
hedgehogs, **11**

invasive predators, 24–25

jellyfish, **40**

komodo dragons, **23**

lions, **15**

mice, 13, 30
minks, **25**

omnivores, **8**
owls, **30**

patience, 7, 16, 21, 23, 30
pelicans, **31**
penguins, **42**
pods, 37
poisons, **22–23**, 24, 40

raptors, **28–29**, **30**
rattlesnakes, **22**
red-shouldered hawks, **6**, 7
researchers, 20, **43**
robins, **32**

scorpions, 22
sea eagles, **26**, 27
seals, **16**, **42**
sharks, **34**, 35, **36**
shrews, 7, 23
snakes, **6**, 7, **21**, **22**, **25**
speeds, 18, 32, 33, 36
spiders, **19**
swallows, 32
swifts, 32

teamwork, **14–15**, 37
tiger beetles, **18**
tigers, **10**
tools, 17, **20**

venom, **22**, 23, 40

warthogs, **29**
whales, **38**
wolves, **14**
woodpeckers, 32

About the Author

Josh Gregory has written more than 80 books covering a wide range of subjects. He lives in Chicago, Illinois.